How to Sell Indexed

Using a Supplemental Life Insurance Retirement Plan.

Second Edition

By Michael Bonilla, CPCU

*"Quality is not an act, it is a habit."*

- Aristotle

## Table of Contents

**About The Author** ................................................... 8

**Preface** ..................................................................... 9

**Introduction** ........................................................... 10

   **What is an Indexed Universal Life Insurance Policy?** ............................................................... 12

   **Brief History and Background** ........................... 13

   **What is a Supplemental Life Insurance Retirement Plan?** ................................................ 13

   **Modern Financial Technology** ........................... 14

   **LIRP/SLIRP Pitfalls as Standalone RPs** ............ 17

   **IUL VS VUL** .......................................................... 18

**Taxes and IUL's** ...................................................... 20

   **IRS Recognized Retirement Plans** ..................... 20

   **IRS Life Insurance Codes** ................................... 20

   **College Planning Advantages** ............................ 21

   **Taxable Buckets** ................................................. 22

   **Rule of 72** ........................................................... 23

   **IUL Vs Qualified Plans** ....................................... 24

      But Mike, why not shift all of my funds into an IUL/SLIRP? ................................................... 26

   **Qualifying Tips for IUL/SLIRP** ........................... 27

**IUL Basics** ............................................................... 28

   **Cap Rate** .............................................................. 28

   **Participation Rate** .............................................. 28

   **Investment Floor** ............................................... 29

   **How are my funds invested?** ............................ 29

**Investing Indexes** ................................................. 30
**Indexing Strategies or Crediting** ....................... 31
**Dollar Cost Averaging** ........................................ 31
**How do I sell the IUL/SLIRP?** .......................... 32
**What are the 'Four Major Problems'** ................ 33
**How do I get started in IUL sales?** .................. 34
**Preparation is Key to Success!** ......................... 34
**5 Step Sales Process** ............................................... 36
  **Step 1: Sell the Appointment** ............................. 38
  **Step 2: Sell the Concept** ..................................... 40
    General Fact Finding ............................................. 41
    Explain Your Process ............................................ 41
    Determine a death benefit. ................................... 42
    L.I.F.E. ....................................................................... 43
    D.I.M.E.S ................................................................... 44
    Common Goals with Financial Plans ................... 44
    Common Retirement Concerns ............................ 45
    Explain the planning process. .............................. 46
    Most Common Myth about Retirement Planning ... 48
    If they ask how it works... .................................... 49
    Annual Review Process (Value Add) .................. 50
    My working Hypothesis for Retirement Planning with a SLIRP. ............................................................ 51
    How much money do you need to retire? (Dream) .................................................................... 51
    Begin to set the stage ............................................ 52
    The Big Tax Question ............................................ 53

Why do taxes go up?..................................................56
What is the current National Debt?.......................56
What happens if the debt keeps going up?..............56
Ask yourself with $20T in debt, what do you think the likelihood of the taxes going up are? Low or High?.................................................57
Four Legged Stool traditional sources of retirement income...............................................57
What if they ask for a price?..................................58
Set Up Expectations..............................................58

**Step 3: Sell the Medical & Conditional Receipt of Insurance ..........................................................60**
Recap.....................................................................60
Recommendation...................................................60
Sell Medical Exam..................................................61
Sell Conditional Receipt of Insurance......................62
What if they ask for a price, again?........................62

**Step 4: Present the offer and deliver policy.......63**
**Step 5: Follow Up on accounts not sold..............64**
**CASE STUDY ........................................................65**
But Mike, do people really live to 100?...................68
Why to think about Single Pay Premium or Re-allocating savings into an IUL?.............................69
How long do you want to live?...............................71
What if I get sick and live too long/too short?........72
How much money will I have in a LIRP when I retire?.................................................................74

    Past performance is not a measure of future performance. ............................................................. 74

    Explain how it works in Detail. ................................ 78

**Closing the Sale** ............................................................. 80

    Should we use an Increasing or level death benefit? ................................................................... 81

    Should we Overfund the policy? ............................. 82

    When does a policy MEC? Modified Endowment Contracts .............................................................. 82

    What about Premium Financing? ............................ 83

    Do I need a life insurance trust LIT/ILIT? ............... 83

    Don't be 'that' guy. .................................................... 84

    Dealing with Stakeholders: Advisors, Accountants and Attorneys ................................... 85

**Typical Newbie Mistakes** ............................................. 89

    Other Considerations ................................................. 90

**Other Sales Strategies** ................................................ 92

**Index of Questions** ...................................................... 94

**Sales Rules** .................................................................... 96

**Summation** .................................................................. 105

## About The Author

How can I help? It's a rather simple creed, but it's mine. This is the reason why I choose to be a writer. I write not to inspire, I write to help others pick up some valuable information that I have learned throughout my career in the insurance industry. My job with these books is rather rudimentary, I am not writing this book to tell you how to think nor tell you what to think, my job with this book is simply to give you something to think about. If I can successfully do that, if I can achieve that, then in essence all I have to do is light the spark. That spark of creativity that eventually turns into a fire and then you fan the flames and that fire can become a roaring blaze.

# Preface

Take a second to think about what we are selling. We are in a very unusual industry. If I do my job correctly, I have not only convinced you to face your own mortality, but to invest in your own death. That being said, my goal with this book is to help you move the dial with your life sales. Maybe you can glean a new phrase, a new question and or some slick statement from this book to adjust your process. Selling is not an exact science, but more of an art form. Selling requires a lot of creativity and a tremendous amount of dedication to your craft and process. This book is a lot of theory backed by trial and error with selling all types of insurance products. This book is also a lot of practical application and process oriented thoughts.

# Introduction

There are many different ways to sell an Indexed Universal Life Policy. This book will walk you through how to leverage a Supplemental Life Insurance Retirement Plan by using an Indexed Universal Life insurance policy. This presentation style isn't for beginners and takes practice to master. It's more of a general framework. You're going to need to fill in the details.

What I've found is that most consumers appreciate the education. So in this book you'll find that we focus a lot on education and leverage that time spent by educating a client. We do a needs analysis and create a customized solution, assuming that the client needs a SLIRP based on what we find during the qualifying process.

After reading this book you should have a more comprehensive understanding the following:

1. How an Indexed Universal Life insurance policy is supposed to work.
2. Understanding how the IUL fits within a client portfolio.
3. Why you should sell IUL's and why clients may need them.
4. Common Objections and ways around them.
5. How an IUL can bridge gaps in retirement plans.
6. Possible Tax Implications for a client.
7. The Pros and Cons of using life insurance as part of a retirement plan.
8. A simple process for selling life insurance.

As we talk about IUL's remember a lot of the work we have to do is setting the stage properly. Traditional pension systems are failing and predicted to have near and long term short falls. So, as a normal person who hopes to retire someday, how can we take advantage of current laws and financial technology? How can we leverage insurance products to tip the scales of retirement in our favor?

# What is an Indexed Universal Life Insurance Policy?

"An **indexed universal life** insurance policy gives the policy holder the opportunity to allocate cash value amounts to either a fixed account or an equity **index** account. **Indexed** policies offer a variety of popular **indexes** to choose from, such as the S&P 500 and the Nasdaq 100." – Investopedia

In other terms, a client is purchasing a life insurance policy that also has investment components that accumulates cash value.

A more consumer facing explanation... "What happened to the value of the 401K and the stock market in 2008?" Trillions of dollars in value were lost in the span of months. Every 10 to 20 years or so the market place of ideas creates a new and more robust form of retirement vehicle or retirement strategy. The market expands, contracts and then adjusts.

## Brief History and Background

Indexed Universal Life Insurance was offered first by Transamerica in 1997 and is now currently offered by over 34 life insurance companies. The IUL is probably the fastest growing product in the financial services sector and is evolving to meet market needs. An indexed universal life insurance plan was the offshoot or next evolution in the family of universal life insurance.

The product overall is evolving constantly to meet accumulation concerns and distribution concerns. Each year we see new rate caps, new interest rate locks, different indexes, changing death benefit options, etc. The predecessor to the IUL was the VUL or variable universal life insurance policy.

## What is a Supplemental Life Insurance Retirement Plan?

A SLIRP is a retirement plan that allows you flexible contributions, flexible distributions, provides a tax free death benefit, provides assistance if you become disabled, provides assistance if you need nursing care, allows you to immediately vest, provides tax free income potential, allows for upside market participation and avoids any losses from a down stock market. For example, let's say you have a really great year this year (financially) you can choose to put more money into your retirement plan. Let's say the opposite happens and money becomes a little tight, the SLIRP gives you the added flexibility of choosing to put in a little less each month.

Think of a SLIRP as an 'in addition to' product to compliment an overall retirement plan by filling gaps where traditional retirement plans fall short. A SLIRP is not a standalone one fits all retirement solution. It's a great addition to an overall retirement plan and not meant to be the sole retirement plan for an insured.

## Modern Financial Technology

Financial technology is just like any other kind of technology. There is old tech and there is new or modern tech. Indexed UL is the most modern financial/retirement technology the market has created. As the government implements new tax plans and new exemptions, the market adjusts. (See chart below)

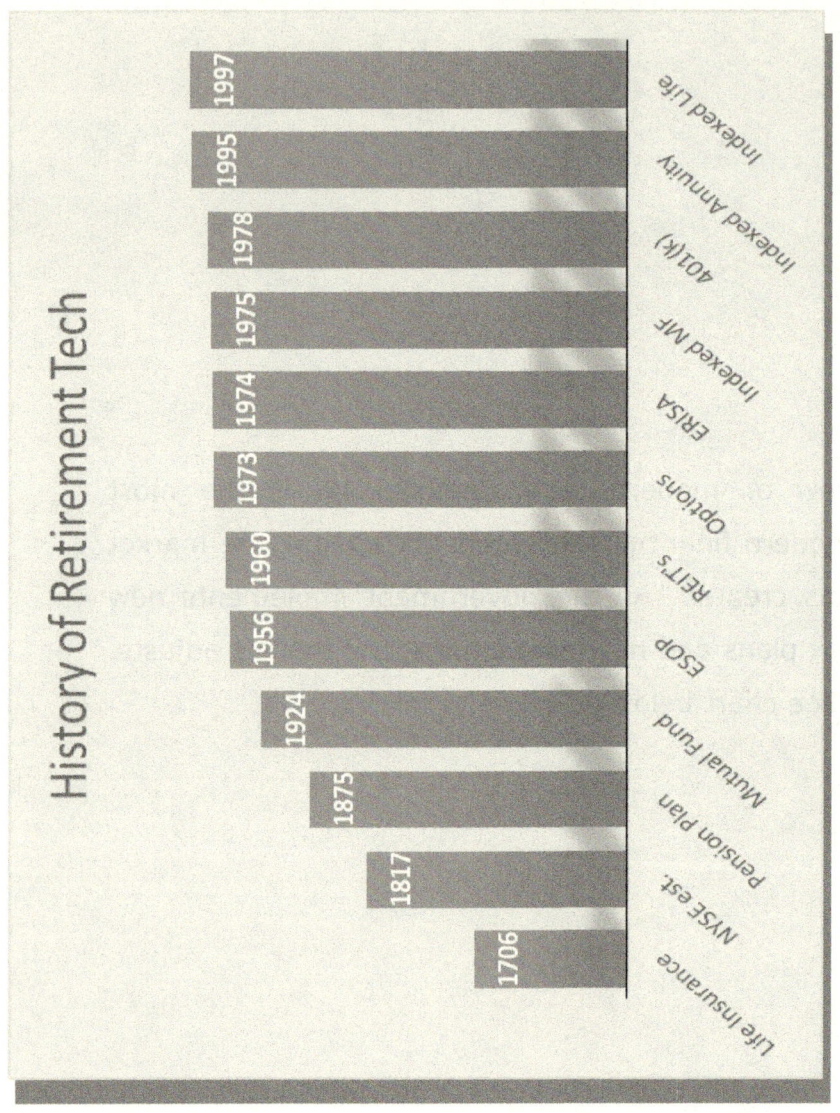

# LIRP/SLIRP Pitfalls as Standalone RPs

But Mike, if I can limit market risk and not pay taxes why shouldn't I dump every possible dollar into this system? Overall, my stance on life insurance in general is somewhat more conservative than most life agents. Here are the four main reasons why.

1. Doesn't allow a client to maximize earnings, because there is a ceiling on earnings or rate cap. (See Chart Below IUL vs VUL)
2. Cost of Insurance can increase diminishing policy gains or requiring the client to increase yearly premiums to maintain earnings stability.
3. It's questionable whether the government will continue to allow these IRC codes to exist with the same language.
4. Policy Loans may or may not have interest rate lock-ins or 'wash' features.

Fundamentally, I believe an IUL is not suited for a standalone retirement solution. Don't put all of your eggs into one basket. An IUL/SLIRP will compliment and fill gaps in an existing traditional retirement plan. I'll explain my reasons in the book and how an IUL compliments an overall retirement plan and fills a lot of gaps. The best way to think of an IUL is that of a gap filler.

## IUL VS VUL

Why isn't the IUL a standalone solution? Well, firstly it doesn't outperform it's more risky variable universal counterpart. If you compare the last 100 years of S&P 500 data an IUL will produce around 6% in return on average and the VUL will produce around 7.5% return. (See chart below)

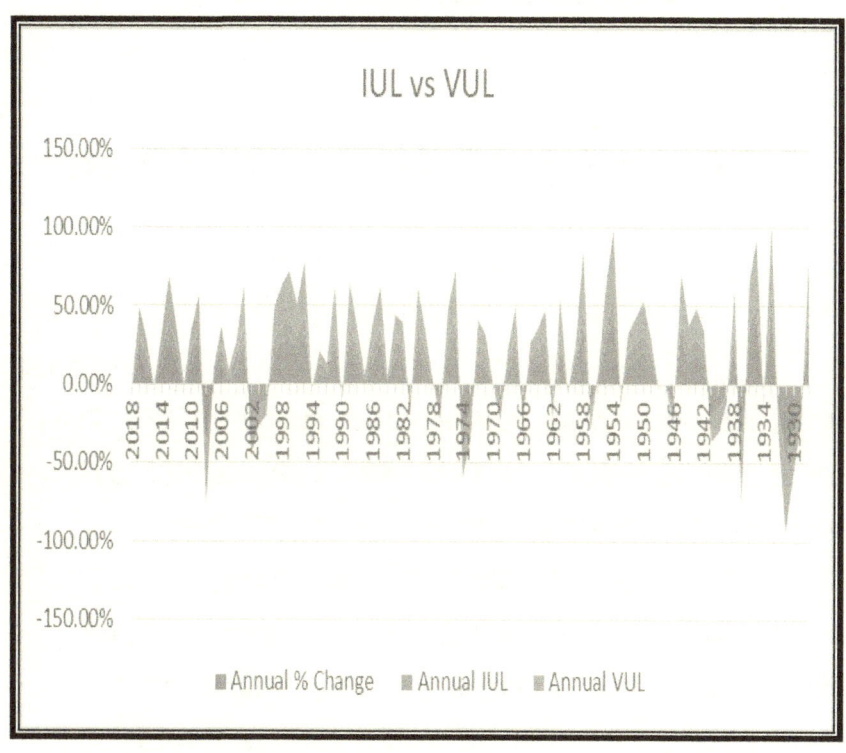

That being said, the reason why I'm a proponent of an IUL over a VUL is the fact that a VUL often requires being wrapped into a life insurance trust. Also, the VUL has **unlimited** risk exposure. Being that I'm in the insurance industry I tend to prefer instruments that hedge against risk. So, theoretically the IUL will underperform by about 18% or so, but that is a pass thru 'tax' which pays for your investment floor.

# Taxes and IUL's

## IRS Recognized Retirement Plans

If you were to follow this hyperlink, (https://www.irs.gov/retirement-plans/plan-sponsor/types-of-retirement-plans) you will find a list of officially recognized retirement plans by the IRS. They are as follows IRAs, Roth IRAs, 401(k) Plans, 403(b) Plans, SIMPLE IRA Plans, SEP Plans, SARSEP Plans, Payroll Deduction IRAs, Profit-Sharing Plans, Defined Benefit Plans, Money Purchase Plans, Employee Stock Ownership Plans (ESOPs), Government Plans and 457 Plans. What do you not see on this list? Two words... Life insurance.

## IRS Life Insurance Codes

This is a sales book. So, I don't plan on getting into the granular Internal Revenue Code. If you are interested as to the actual codes that pertain to life insurance, please feel free to look up the following on the IRS website.

- **IRC 72**

- **IRC 7702**

- **IRC 1.01(a)(2)**

## College Planning Advantages

For the purposes of college funding and preparation, the United States government does not include cash value in life insurance as an investment or asset. This means that an insured could funnel money out of other investments or cash into an Indexed Universal Life Policy to <u>possibly</u> obtain favorable treatment for college financial aid, make sure to check with your CPA and student aid advisor. Below is a referenced copy of the **FAFSA 2018-2019** student application form page number 10, section titled **Investments do not include**.

> **Investments do not include** the home you live in, the value of life insurance, retirement plans (401[k] plans, pension funds, annuities, non-education IRAs, Keogh plans, etc.) or cash, savings and checking accounts already reported in questions 41 and 90.

Did you know that certain life insurance policies might put your children in a more favorable financial situation to obtain Federal Student Aid?

## Taxable Buckets

When we look at investments there are three buckets we can group every investment into; Currently Taxable, Deferred Taxable and Tax Free (Tax Advantaged).

**Taxable:** Stocks, Bonds, Real Estate, Mutual Funds, Option Contracts, Silver, Sold, Etc.

**Tax Deferred:** 401k, IRA, 403B, Pension Plans, KEOGH, TSP, SEP IRA and Annuities.

**Tax Free:** 529 Plans and Cash Value loaned from Life Insurance

**\*Author Notation:** 529 Plans and Life Insurance can be taxable if not executed correctly. It's important to talk with plan administrators to prevent this from happening.

## Rule of 72

Believe it or not Albert Einstein once called the effects of compound interest the 'Eighth wonder of the world.' The rule of 72 is a simple calculation to determine the time it takes for an investment to double based on a specified interest rate. Why is this important? Well, this rule is a rather easy way to not only explain, but to illustrate to clients how soon they need to start saving for retirement. **72 Divided by the Rate of Return equals the number of years to double.** (See Chart Below)

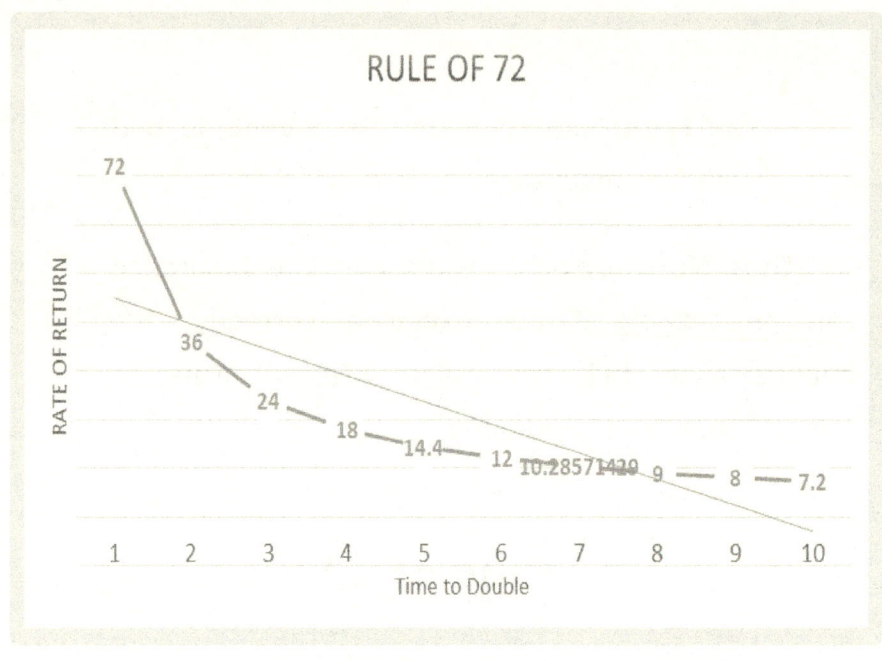

## IUL Vs Qualified Plans

An IUL is not a qualified account and a retirement plan described by the IRS is not life insurance. That being said, here are some of the key distinctions comparable and ways to look at a SLIRP versus a qualified plan. **It's important to note that this is for educational purposes for the reader and not meant to be client facing or represented as an endorsement for comparing an IUL and qualified plan during a client presentation.**

|  | IUL | Qualified Plans |
| --- | --- | --- |
| Distributions | Not Taxed | Taxed as income |
| Early Withdrawal Penalty | No | 10% Tax before age 59 1/2 |
| Option to take Lump Sum | Yes | Yes |
| Required Minimum Distribution | No | 10% tax after 70 1/2 |
| Pre-tax Contribution | No | Yes, on some accounts. |
| Ability to Annuitize distribution | No | Maybe |
| Management Fee | Yes | Yes |
| Required to be employed to contribute | No | Yes, for most. |
| Portable | Yes | Yes, rollovers possible. |
| Employer Contributions | Rare | Yes, possible. |
| Ability to take loans against | Yes | Yes |

| accounts. | | |
|---|---|---|
| Investment Floor | Yes | No |
| Investment Ceiling | Yes | No |
| Guaranteed Lifetime Income | Possible | No |
| Guaranteed Minimum Fixed Account % | Yes, 3% | No |
| Tax free Death Benefit | Yes | No |
| Long Term Care Rider | Yes | No |
| Disability Waiver | Yes | No |
| Critical Illness Protection | Yes | No |
| Disability Income Provisions | Yes | No |

## But Mike, why not shift all of my funds into an IUL/SLIRP?

If you receive a matching component from your employer, why would you give up free money? Mainly, don't put all of your eggs into one basket. Also, from an

Agent standpoint if the life insurance company goes bankrupt, what happens to the life policy? It's uncertain. From an Errors and Omissions perspective it's quite risky to start re-allocating funds into an IUL from a 401k or other qualified account.

## Qualifying Tips for IUL/SLIRP

Who is the right fit for an IUL? Well, start with the basics. Does the client have an ongoing need for life insurance? Is the client age 20 to 45? Does the client have favorable medical underwriting? Has the client shown a history of saving and investing? What kind of investments do you have currently that are 100% market risk free? Do you have any investments that give you upside potential, eliminate downside market risk and provide you tax free distributions? Have you ever considered paying your insurance premium in full? But Mike, why would I ever do that? Your earning potential when paying in full can increase.

# IUL Basics

In this part of the chapter we are going to cover how the IUL works and the basic structure along with some of the key sellable benefits or features. If you are currently selling Life Insurance, you might want to skip this part.

## Cap Rate

The 'Cap' rate is basically just your ceiling or upward earnings potential. For instance, most IUL's have a 'Cap' Rate of around 10%. Meaning that you can earn up to 10% per year.

## Participation Rate

This is the percentage of the cap you can participate in. For instance, if you have a 10% cap rate and a 100% participation rate when the market goes up you can achieve up to 10%. If the market goes up 8%, you get 8%. If the market goes up 1% you get 1%. So, on and so forth.

## Investment Floor

An Investment floor is simply the bottom of your risk. For instance, IUL's have 'floors' of 0% on almost all IUL policies. Which means in the event that the index goes below 0% you lose nothing. For example, if the S&P 500 drops by 50% in a single year, you lose nothing.

## How are my funds invested?

This is somewhat of an over simplification of how it works, but here is basically how it works. A portion of your money is invested in your fixed accounts producing a guaranteed minimum amount of interest, typically around 4%. The outstanding portion that is not in the fixed account is invested in the indexed accounts. (See chart below)

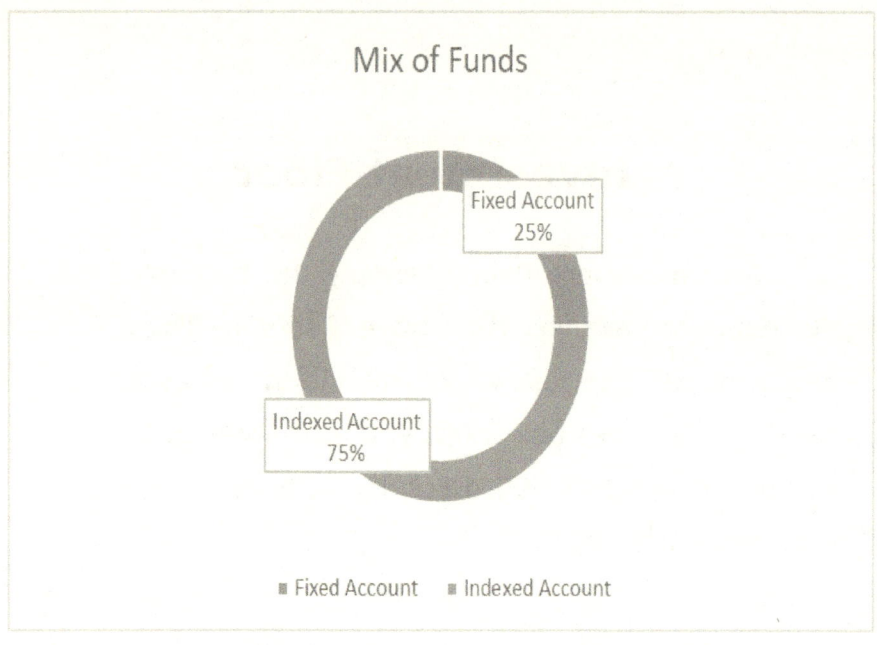

## **Investing Indexes**

Generally speaking every life insurance company utilizes the same half a dozen or so indexes. For the purposes of this book we will keep this rather short and sweet.

- S&P 500
- Nasdaq 100
- Russell 2000
- International Funds

## Indexing Strategies or Crediting

Generally, most insurance companeis use the same half a dozen or so crediting strategies as well. For the purposes of this book we will keep this rather short and sweet.

- Daily Averaging
- Point to Point Monthly
- Point to Point Annual
- Point to Average

## Dollar Cost Averaging

DCA is a very simple investing strategy that involves investing the same amount of money over time in sequential intervals. For instance, investing in one stock over 10 years but putting in the same $100 each month. An easy way to think about DCA is as a long term passive investing strategy. See chart below.

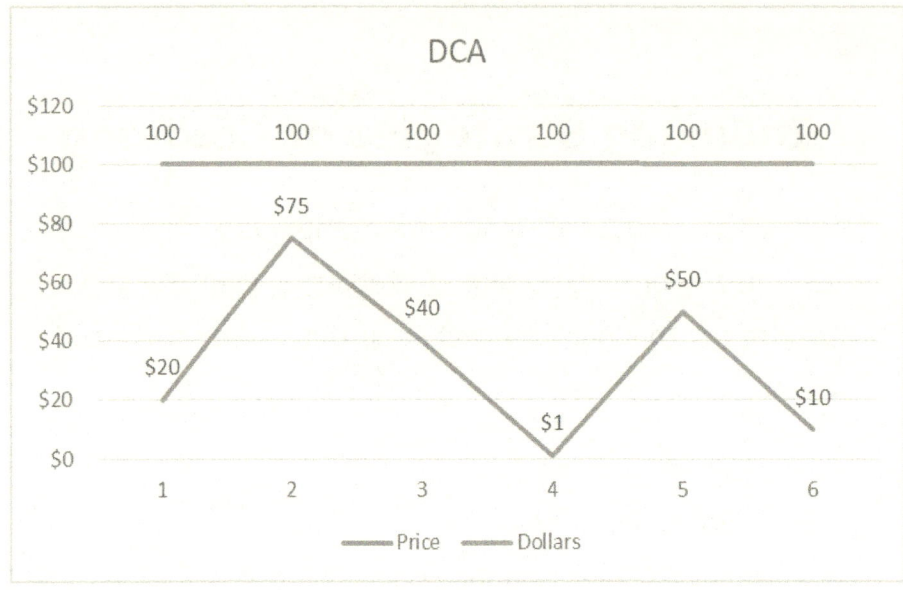

## How do I sell the IUL/SLIRP?

1. Determine a Death Benefit
2. Understand a Client's Retirement 'Dream'
3. Set a retirement Age goal and income goal to meet the 'dream'.
4. Analyze a Person's Current Retirement funding.
5. Does the Retirement Plan Address the Four Major Problems?
6. Does the current funding meet the 'dream'?
7. Show how an IUL/SLIRP can fill the gaps.

## What are the 'Four Major Problems'...

When planning for inevitable retirement we all face the same four core dilemmas. These are the four dilemmas where insurance can step in and round out a retirement account. See below.

1. You live too long and outlive their savings.
2. You live too long and get sick.
3. You live too short get sick and rack up medical debt.
4. You live long and become disabled young.

By considering adding a supplement retirement plan to an existing retirement plan you provide a vehicle (Indexed Universal Life) to protect a client against all of these problems that traditional retirement planning fails to do in an efficient/effective manner.

## How do I get started in IUL sales?

Don't force the issue. Don't go into a life prospecting call thinking about closing an IUL each and every time, go into the call thinking about client acquisition first and foremost. Life insurance is a numbers game pure and simple. The home runs will come, play fundamental baseball and focus on base hits. To be great at something you first must learn to be consistent.

## Preparation is Key to Success!

1. Have all supporting documents in order of how you want to present them to a client. Each client is different and needs to be handled with different levels of consideration.
2. Make sure to write down these four questions and check them off as you present.
3. Part of the Art of Persuasion is understanding which of your 'slick' statements work on which people. Everyone responds differently and that's why you have to practice so you learn when to say what and when to pause and listen.

**4.** Make sure to ask a lot of open ended questions, actively listen and then ask specific follow questions.

# 5 Step Sales Process

When presenting insurance proposals I always used to have a twostep meeting process. The first meeting I would qualify, fact find and discover needs. The first meeting was all about selling myself, my company, my insurance carriers and selling the next meeting for the product unveiling. This meeting was important to plant seeds, establish myself as an expert and garner time to run illustrations with multiple offerings. Ideally, we would also discover and uncover underlying concerns, questions and ways to weigh needs/wants. The second meeting was the unveiling of the product and sole purpose would be to sell the explain the solution for earlier stated uncovered problem, medical exam, sign the app and get a check for conditional receipt of insurance.

Step 1: Sell the Appointment

Step 2: Sell the Concept

Step 3: Sell the Medical & Conditional Receipt of Insurance

Step 4: Present the offer and deliver policy

## Step 5: Follow Up on Accounts Not Closed

## Step 1: Sell the Appointment

During the first meet and greet is when you build rapport and establish the relationship with the prospect. This is the singularly most important meeting you can ever have with a client, from the second you open your mouth you are selling. For newer agents this can be the most arduous part of the process. I'm not talking about setting appointments with family member and getting a top '25' list. I'm talking about organically prospecting and selling in social settings without alienating friends, family and co-workers.

- Build Rapport
- Sell yourself
- Set up a meeting to discuss needs and wants.
- Get to know the person.
- Get the person to know you.

Don't show your hand before you play your hand. The biggest mistake I see most agents make during the prospecting phase is that they tend to talk shop to prospects and not talk about the person. Yes, I understand that an IUL is a very exciting concept. But, people don't care about what you know until they know that you care.

So, how do we do that? The simplest way is to ask questions about the person. The more we can know about a prospect the more we can customize an offering to meet the specific needs of that prospect. People generally speaking all talk about their favorite subject in life, themselves. So, talk about them. Figure out what they do for a living, or what they do for down time.

- What do you do for a living?
- How long have you been doing that/it?
- What do you like about what you do?
- What do you do really well?

Have you ever heard of a term called incidental similarities? It's a quite simple sales/psychological term. At Disneyland every name tag has the name of the employee's home town on it. Why? Because, instantly it may make an attachment or have some kind of meaning between the employee and the consumer.

## Step 2: Sell the Concept

During the first meeting is when you have to accomplish a few goals. This is the meeting where we have to establish the need for life insurance. We need to plant seeds and expectation and help the client understand how the process works. Life insurance is an exclusive product and not everyone will qualify. As an expert we do not recommend this product to everyone who can fog a mirror. This meeting we spend time qualifying the client, which involves first determining and focusing on the death benefit.

General Underwriting Fact Finding

Explain Your Process

Calculate a Death Benefit.

Establish as an authority and subject matter expert.

Explain the Planning Process.

Explain the Application Process.

Needs Analysis and Fact Finding.

Problem or Opportunity Discovery.

Client Buys-In to Problem.

Possible Solution (next appointment)

## General Fact Finding

Fact finding is crucial for setting up presentations for qualified prospects. What do you have now that acts like life insurance? Do you have life insurance through your work? If so, how much? Who did you plan on having as the beneficiary of the policy? Why? Height, weight, DOB, SSN, etc. Have you recently applied for life insurance? If so, what was the outcome?

## Explain Your Process

Well John, as we design your plan we are going to gather quite a bit of information, because there is no such thing as a good deal for the wrong insurance policy. Our process albeit somewhat detailed is done in that way so we can create you a truly customized offering to fit the coverage to your specific needs. Our job is not just to sell you insurance, but to make sure we spend the time to educate you as to how it works for your situation.

## Determine a death benefit.

How often do you come across a competitor's Declaration Page and wonder how that amount of insurance was arrived at? $250,000 or $500,000... well it's at least a nice round number of insurance. But, why is that your number? The key fundamental need for underwriting a life insurance policy is a need for life insurance, so we need to determine a death benefit. With a Supplement Life Insurance Retirement Plan use a formula that fits your flow. You can use the Human Life Value Approach which uses the person's income earning potential over a certain amount of years.

- Human Life Value Approach
- 10x Income Approach
- 5x Income Approach
- L.I.F.E
- D.I.M.E.S

Typically, my lead in with any of these systems was the same. Did you have an amount of insurance in mind or were you looking for some guidance? I'd say from experience 90% of the prospects I spoke with would ask for some kind of guidance. Even if they had a number in mind I would always ask a follow up question, "Great! How'd you arrive at that amount of insurance?" Remember, there is no wrong way to ask for a death benefit not a correct way. There are merely just different ways to ask.

## L.I.F.E.

There is no perfect system for determining a death benefit. The reason I chose to use the LIFE system, it almost eliminates price as an objection. Why? Because, we know have a detailed accounting of income, expenses, etc. The LIFE system is easy to illustrate on a whiteboard or piece of paper. It's a system that as a new agent was quite easy for me to pick up and run with.

The LIFE system goes as follows...

1. Loans (Outstanding Debt)
2. Income
3. Funeral Costs (10,000 to 20,000)
4. Emergency Expenses or Educational Costs

It's a very simple formula and allows you to learn a lot about the person you are trying to insure. It helps you understand purchasing behavior. Ask yourself how can you customize your offering without knowing specific details about your client? I've seen some reps just pitch generic loan amounts to clients and try to see the corresponding rates.

## D.I.M.E.S

The DIMES system is similar to the LIFE system in that it covers every aspect of your life and expense structure. The DIMES system goes as follows:

- Debt (Credit Card, Student Loans, etc.)
- Income (10X Incomes or until youngest child is 18)
- Mortgage (Outstanding Mortgage Amount)
- Education Fund (50,000 per child)
- Savings or Safety Net (Optional)

## Common Goals with Financial Plans

With designing your financial plan what I've found is that everyone has the same goal. To grow their money as large and as fast as possible. Because, there's never a good time to start saving and you can never retire too early.

But, as we grow older and get closer to our retirement age we shift our concern from growth to preservation of capital. How soon can I access my money and how much do I have left to access? Is my money protected?

## Common Retirement Concerns

Would it be fair to say that most people have similar retirement concerns? Sure. Well John, most of my clients are primarily concerned with these three BIG concerns during retirement. Do you mind if I share those with you?

1. The first concern is, "Will I have enough money during retirement?" Why? Because, no one wants to outlive their savings.
2. The second concern is, "God forbid I should pass away prematurely, will my death be a financial burden to my family?"

3. The third concern is, "What if I were to get sick or in critical care due to an accident? How will that affect my finances?"

## Explain the planning process.

As we get older we tend to take on less risk in our investment portfolio as we begin to liquidate funds. You've done the responsible thing and saved up all this money, now is the time to protect it. But, what if I had a way to invest your money in the stock market where you could never lose money if the stock market collapsed like it did in 2008? Sounds too good to be true, right? Well, here's the catch. Firstly, we have to make sure you qualify for this product, because any people do not qualify. Secondly, the tradeoff for this product is that although you will never lose money from market crashes, you are capped in the amount you can make. This is called a ceiling on your earnings per year. For instance, if the market grows by 15% you can participate in most of the upside, up until you reach 10%. If the market crashes and loses 15%, you lose 0%, this is called a floor. In essence, the life insurance company and investment firm take the upside difference, but protect you against any possible downside.

The three phases of retirement planning (see chart below):

- Contribution (Put Money In)
- Accumulation (Grow that Money)
- Distribution (Liquidate)

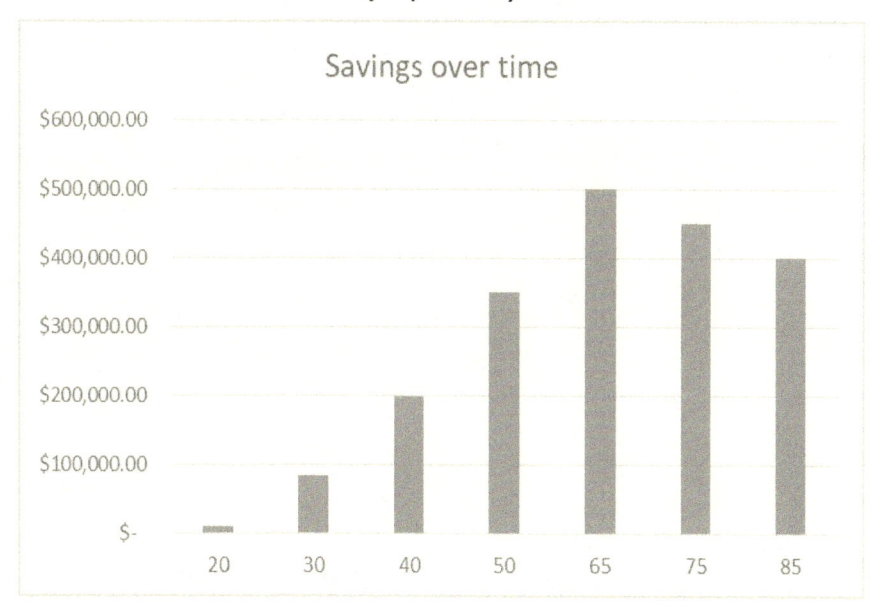

**Savings over time**

| Age | Savings |
|---|---|
| 20 | $- |
| 30 | ~$100,000.00 |
| 40 | $200,000.00 |
| 50 | ~$350,000.00 |
| 65 | $500,000.00 |
| 75 | ~$450,000.00 |
| 85 | $400,000.00 |

Would it be fair to say that as we get older we look to protect our money more than we look to grow our money? We trade rate of return for protectio from risk? Typically, most of my clients tend shift their investments into more conservative investments as they get older. We work our whole life to build a nest egg and eventually it becomes time to protect that egg. (See Chart Below)

**Rate of Return vs Age**

| Age | Rate |
|---|---|
| 20 | 12% |
| 30 | 10% |
| 40 | 8% |
| 50 | 7% |
| 65 | 5% |
| 75 | 4% |
| 85 | 3% |

# Most Common Myth about Retirement Planning

When you retire, will your taxes go up or go down? It's hard to say. Most people will be making less money but at the same time your deductions might as well. Most people think that when they retire their tax rate will go down. But, remember you have less dependents and most likely less deductions.

## If they ask how it works...

With a traditional 401k or qualified retirement account or even just owning stocks or bonds you accept unlimited upside potential for gains and also unlimited downside potential for losses.

With a Supplemental LIRP you are limited to earning up to 10% (Each Company is Different) per year but, unlike investing a traditional retirement plan you have ZERO downside risk potential. This is what's called an investment floor. Which simply means the least you can earn is 0% and the most is 10%. It will out-perform your savings outcome but most likely somewhat or slightly under-perform your 401K.

There are also components or riders we can add on the policy that will kick in if you should become disabled or need nursing home care due to an accident.

Every person has the same fundamental goal when it comes to putting money away for retirement. Ideally, during the next twenty years until you retire, you want your money to do what? To grow as large as possible. With traditional plans you put money away for 40 years and have less take home pay. At the end of 40 years you are hoping the tax rate is less than it is when you put away that money.

## Annual Review Process (Value Add)

As a value add to my clients I make a commitment to reviewing their sub-accounts and investment accounts to make sure that we are on track to our goals. In the event that we are having a great year and you have a little extra money we can think about overfunding. It's important to remember that people like to be thought of as individuals. So, make sure to ask and not force the issue. Some clients don't want to meet once a year. Some clients would prefer once a quarter. After writing a long term client with a new product I found this out the hard way. I gave my usual shtick of, "Most of my clients like to plan on meeting once per year to review…" To which he replied bluntly, "I'm not most of your clients." Always ask, John given your unique situation how often would you like to follow up and review your progress? Once a year? Twice a year?

# My working Hypothesis for Retirement Planning with a SLIRP.

The overall hypothesis that I use with this strategy is that the client will want an additional blanket of protection. A blanket of protection against tax increases, broader flexibility for distributions, long term care in case they become ill and life insurance in case they should pass away. On top of that we can minimize all downside market risk by indexing.

# How much money do you need to retire? (Dream)

When you ask most people what is the common answer? A million dollars. Okay, how did you come to that amount? Well, it's a lot of money. I think I could retire off of that. This from what I have found is a great place to start. Now we have a number in mind we can probe further and get a yearly retirement income goal and from there a retirement age goal. (Both of which will help develop your presentation) Well, let me ask you something Bob...

- When you retire do you want your standard of living to go up, down or stay about the same?
- How do you want to live out your retirement?
- Do you want to travel?
- Leave some money behind for family/charities?
- At what age do you want to retire?
- Do you want your home paid off by the time you retire?

## Begin to set the stage

When looking at your Retirement Plan there are three types of investments buckets. Where do you want to put your money? Do you want the government of your grandkids to get your money? With taxes at an all-time 100 year low and debt to GDP at an all-time 200 year high, where do you think taxes are going?

1. **Taxable Investment** – Stocks and Bonus

2. **Tax Deferred** – Retirement Accounts. Such as, 401K, IRA, 403B, etc.
3. **Tax Free Investment** – Life Insurance and 529 Plans

Along with taxable benefits, flush out any possible underlying concerns about long term care or disability. About 50% of adults between 40 and 60 are three generation dependent households in America. That being said, find out how that effects the insured on a daily basis and on a stress basis as well.

## The Big Tax Question

The current US Top Federal Tax rate is about 39.5%. What do you think it'll be in 30 years when you retire? Do you think taxes will go up, down or stay the same? The answer is we have no idea. We have to make an educated guess. With Taxable and Tax Deferred investments you take on virtually unlimited investment risk and worst of all have no idea what the tax risk you face when it comes time to take your distributions.

Do you think taxes will go up or down? Consider this. At the highest point in US history the top federal tax rate was over 90% of your income. If you were to gamble or place a bet? Would you place a bet on taxes going up? Staying the same? Or going down long term?

**U.S. FEDERAL INCOME TAX RATES 1913-2016**

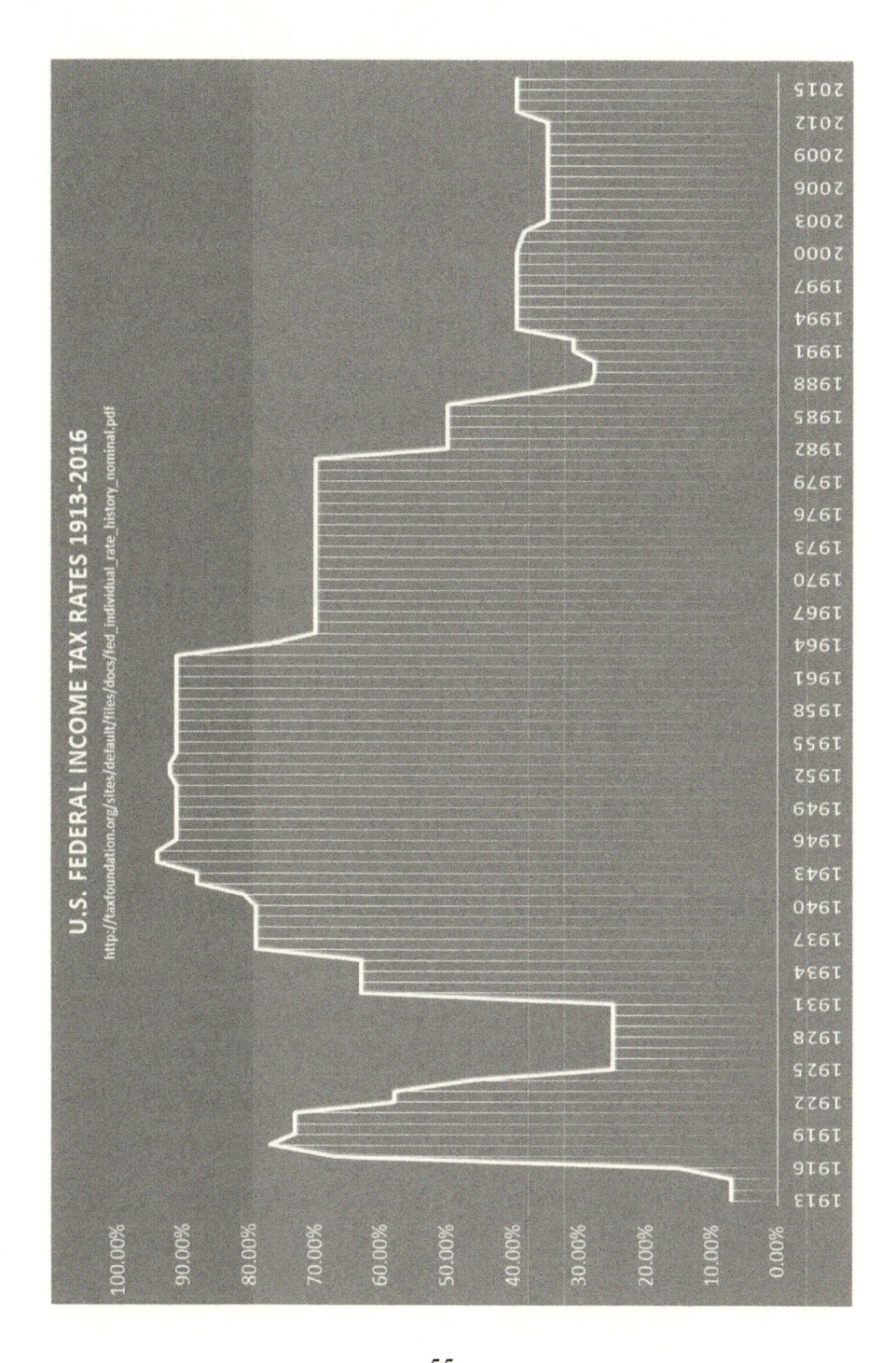

http://taxfoundation.org/sites/default/files/docs/fed_individual_rate_history_nominal.pdf

## Why do taxes go up?

The main reason we need taxes is to fund the government and pay outstanding national debt obligations. So, if you look at the historical debt to tax revenue we as a country are at an all-time high.

## What is the current National Debt?

As of 2015 the government has managed to accumulate about Twenty Trillion dollars in Federal debt. Or $170,378 per Taxpayer.

## What happens if the debt keeps going up?

Hyperinflation. Money can become worthless. Remember, reading about World War 2 and seeing photos of Germans burning money for warmth? When too much money chases too few goods the price drastically escalates.

# Ask yourself with $20T in debt, what do you think the likelihood of the taxes going up are? Low or High?

Most sane people would think the likelihood of taxes going up in the face of that much debt are high, especially when seeing that taxes were for a long time over 90%.

# Four Legged Stool traditional sources of retirement income

Around 75 years ago the greatest generation really figured it all out. Private companies created pension systems, social security was created and the personal savings rate was fairly high. Today, that story has changed somewhat.

- **Pension** – about 7 percent of employers offer a traditional company pension. Compared to 60% in the 1980's. Most companies offer a 401k.
- **Social Security**
    o Less Workers per Retirees taking benefits.
    o Life Expectancy is increasing.

- **Personal Savings** – Interest rates for savings accounts, even large savings accounts are usually less than 1%.
- Company **Life Policy** Equal to 1 year salary.

## What if they ask for a price?

Whom is the expert? Is the insured/prospect the expert or are you the expert. Some life agents are so gun hoe they just throw out non-binding numbers after a five minute conversation with the client. If you've been in this industry for more than a minute, you know a person can look health on the outside but might have something going-on on the inside we cannot see.

## Set Up Expectations

As we start to put together some options for you. Would you be open to the idea of looking at a life insurance plan that acts as a 'tax free retirement vehicle'? Wait for an answer. Where do we go from here? What are my next steps?

**\*Author Notation -** This is a strategy called

asking for the ask. I'm not asking for the sale per se. I'm asking the client for permission to ask for the sale. I'm putting the onus on the client to make a decision and also buy-in to the idea.

# Step 3: Sell the Medical & Conditional Receipt of Insurance

The third step is the easy step where you take all the information gathered and re-digest it with a solution in mind to fit the client. This meeting is solely about presenting the solution and then getting the signature on the app and a check. It's really that simple.

## Recap

Recap the last meeting and what was discussed. If you sell on value and focus on the death benefit there shouldn't be much commotion about price or being the right fit. Remember, if the client sticks with you thru the process then they are at the very least open to hearing what you have to say.

## Recommendation

Make your professional recommendation to suit the needs of the client. Explain how the product works. Explain the illustrations. Explain the break-even analysis, explain the surrender charges. Explain the product and close the application. I'm recommending this insurance company above all the other insurance company's I offer because it is the best to fulfil everything we spoke about in our last meeting and X, Y and Z. Explain target and minimum premium.

## Sell the Medical Exam

Insurance is an exclusive product and thusly we all have an advantage as sales people. Think about it, the only thing that qualifies someone for buying a Mercedes is the money to do so. Life insurance is not like other products. It's not like a bar of soap or a car. It's not something you can walk into a store and are guaranteed to purchase. Explain the process. As your agent I suggest we apply for X amount of insurance thru X insurance company, because X, Y and Z. If you get objections then just explain the process again. I've seen underwriting take 10 days and I've seen it take 30 or 40 or 90 days in some cases to complete. Until we complete this stage in the process nothing gets done, there is no offer. The truth is, I have no idea what you qualify for until we get this medical exam done.

## Sell Conditional Receipt of Insurance

Make sure to obtain a check for the conditional receipt. What is that you ask? Well, during the underwriting which as mentioned could take up to 90 days, we use a 10% premium check to cover that unknown duration. If the underwriting takes 2 days we can apply the difference to the account. But, if the underwriting takes 90 days we are going to need coverage to protect your family. The reason why I recommend we go with this small amount is that the insurance is not guaranteed, but it will provide insurance until the underwriter can make a decision.

## What if they ask for a price, again?

With an IUL we have a target and minimum premium based on the illustrations, so we need to address price for an IUL sale. But, with the caveat that there will be strict medical underwriting.

## Step 4: Present the offer and deliver policy

This part of the book will be rather short. If the client sticks with you through a long process, which serious buyers tend to then this meeting is a payoff of all the diligence. Great news! The life insurance has extended you an offer for an indexed universal life policy with a rating of X. Explain the medical underwriting results and how the process works from this point on. Close out the account.

## Step 5: Follow Up on accounts not sold

This is arguably the most important part of the process. Selling is a rather easy process. Most salespeople tend not to have the best follow up process, me being one of them. Make sure to have a diligent follow up process as sometimes the grass is not always greener on the other side of the fence. The average lead takes 6 follow ups or calls to properly develop into a solid prospect. The average lead not closed has a 25% chance at re-engagement within 6 to 9 months.

# CASE STUDY

### Bobby B.

- DOB 6/15/1970
- Income = $75,000 per year.
- Bob is a single home owner.
- Bob donates 10% of his income to the YMCA.
- Bob has a 401K that he contributes 10% of his income to with a 5% matching component.
- Bob has a savings account balance of $25,000.
- Bob plans on withdrawing Social Security at age 62.
- Bob saves about 5% to 10% of his gross income per year.
- Bob has aspirations to get married one day and travel in his retirement with his future spouse.

### Retirement Goals

1. Retirement Income Goal: $75,000/year
2. Retirement Age Goal: 62

## Where does he stand now?

- At age 62 in 2032, if Social security is still around you can expect to receive a monthly check of **$1,558** or **$18,696** per year.
  *https://www.ssa.gov/oact/quickcalc/index.html
- You currently have $25,000 in Savings. If you continue to save at the same rate you should have around **$137,500** in savings. (Assuming 5% savings per year at 75,000 consistent income).
- Your company offer a 401k which they match up to 5% of pre-tax income, which is great! If we assume a conservative rate of return on your 401k of 5.5% you're estimated accumulation will be **$643,951** by age 62. (Using a calculator but remember it's only theoretical as nothing is guaranteed)
- Bob also has a group term policy thru work for 1 year's salary worth of death benefit that he pays about $25 a month for.

So, the average life span is 78 and you want to retire at 62, which is 16 years. Now, let's say worst case scenario Bob lives to 78. Let's see if you'll have enough money.

(Again along with customizing, assuming the average life span isn't customizing. Try asking open ended questions and specific questions. So, the average life span is 79 for men, would it be reasonable to think you might outlive that?)

That leaves you with $137,500 after tax money, $643,951 of taxable income and a stream of taxable income of $18,696 per year. If we assume you take equal distributions that is $40,246 (401K) and $18,696 of SSI or a combined income of $58,942. Now worst case scenario again. Let's say Bob remains single, his federal tax rate would be 25% plus a state income tax.

So, his net income most likely is around $44,206. If you calculate inflation into that figure in today's dollars he would need a comparable $87,000 per year to have the same purchasing power.

What happens if... (Determine if his current

67

retirement plan meets his retirement income goals/age and if the 4 questions are answered. If either are not met then a SLIRP might be what Bob needs.)

1. You live to 100... $35,642 per year of taxable income.
2. You live to 100 but have to live in a nursing home...
3. You end up in nursing care at a younger age?

If Bob becomes ill or unable to take care of himself most likely he will have to blow through his savings and or take hardship withdrawals on his 401k. If he dies prematurely he does have some life insurance in place to take care of some debt obligations and a funeral.

## But Mike, do people really live to 100?

Yes it happens. We are tabulating life policies to sunset at age 100. Life extending technology will allow people to live longer each year.

*E&O Tip. Never Re-allocate 401k funds into an IUL/VUL if the client is currently receiving matching contributions up to what they receive in matching. Free money is free money.*

## Why to think about Single Pay Premium or Re-allocating savings into an IUL?

So, I get this question a lot. Should my client get into infinite banking or one of these top heavy life products (front loaded)? Considering the rule of 72 and how bank accounts pay 0% interest on a savings account, maybe. If you average the inflation rate over the last 100 years it averages around 3% per year. So, every dollar in a savings account is basically earning you negative 3% interest per year. Here's the thing, you cannot just take your money out of a life insurance policy with zero recourse. The life insurance is meant to mature, it's not a savings account.

**HISTORICAL INFLATION RATES 1914 - 2015**

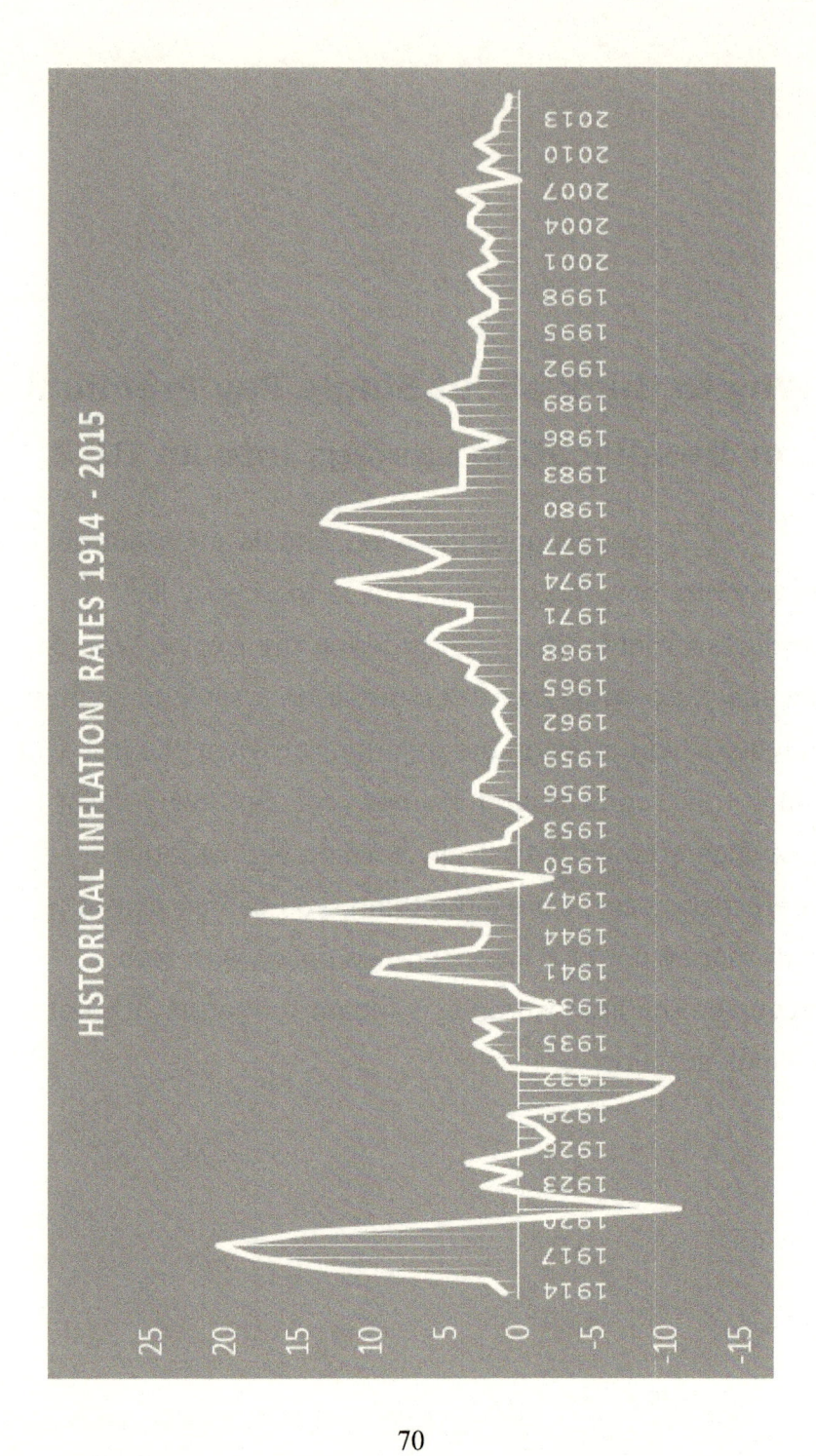

## How long do you want to live?

The average life expectancy is 79 years for men and 81 years for women. When do you want to retire? 62, 65 or 70? For most people the answer is as soon as possible. But, let's say they want to work until 70. How long do you expect to live? In my family I've have had over 4 relatives outlive 100 years of age. I think the highest was 108. Sicilians are very stubborn people.

Remember when you ask a client this question. It's pretty hard to be introspective. But, with life extending technology would it be reasonable to say that you might live into your 90s?

Yes, that might be reasonable. Okay, do you think with your savings at X, your 401k at Y and with Social Security at Z you will have enough money?

What do you want your retirement to look like? Do you want to travel? Start a business? Leave an endowment fund for your great grand kids? I knew my great grandfather and he was around until my mid-twenties. Let me tell you he changed my life.

## What if I get sick and live too long/too short?

What most Financial Planners / Retirement Experts always forget to insure against is what happens if Bob lives long and then gets sick or requires In-home Nursing Care or must be placed into a nursing home? What happens if Bob becomes disable and can no longer work? What's the plan? With an IUL/SLIRP you can fill that gap with cost efficient riders added to the policy.

**Average Annual Nursing Home Charges**

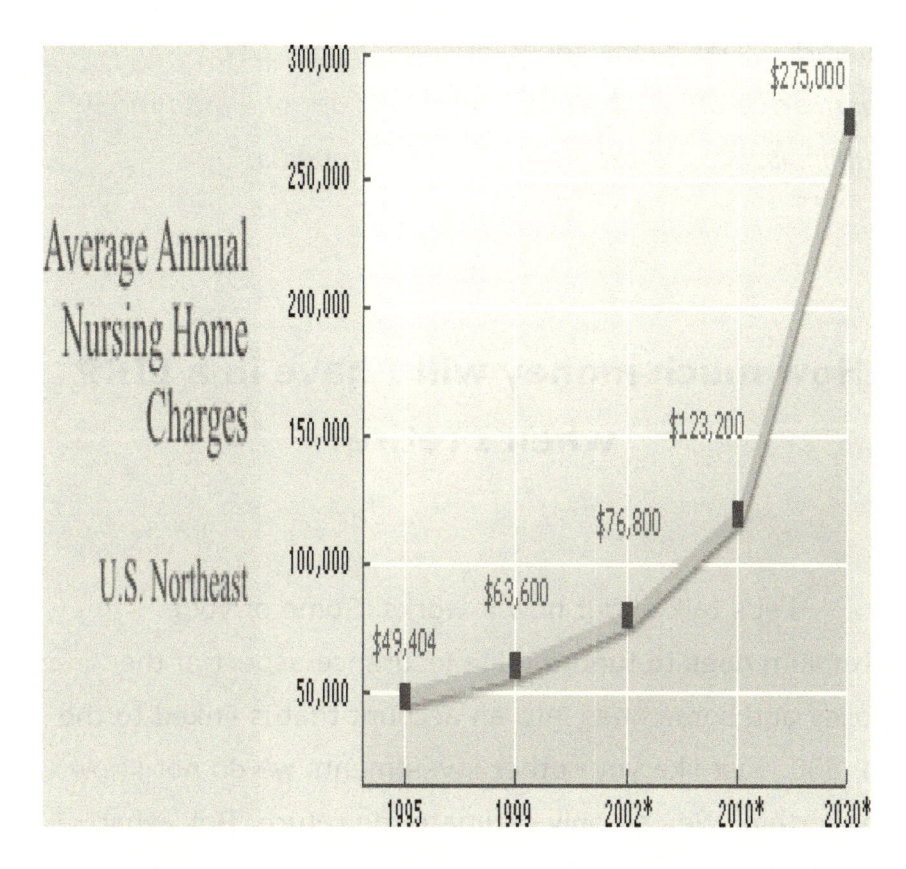

**U.S. Northeast**

- 1995: $49,404
- 1999: $63,600
- 2002*: $76,800
- 2010*: $123,200
- 2030*: $275,000

With your SLIRP, the insurance company doesn't care how you use your money. It's your money. We've also added a feature called a Long term Care rider* to help address any long term care needs (talked about later).

*"Coverage that provides nursing-home *care*, home-health *care*, personal or adult day*care* for individuals above the age of 65 or with a chronic or disabling

73

*condition that needs constant supervision.* **LTC insurance** *offers more flexibility and options than many public assistance programs." – Investopedia.*

## How much money will I have in a LIRP when I retire?

Let's talk about how it works. Some of your premium goes to fund the life insurance aspect of the policy and some goes into an account that is linked to the SP 500. Just like your other investments we do not know for certain. We can only estimate the return. But, what we can guarantee is that the investment account will never lose money due to drops in the stock market.

## Past performance is not a measure of future performance.

When you sit down with a financial advisor 9 times out of ten they tell you just that, because no one has a magic eight ball. But, how does a financial advisor convince you to use a 401K? By past historical performance of the market. How do they convince you to sign up with their firm? Because, they have produced an average of x% of return for clients over the past 100 years.

Although past performance is no indication of future performance people who had an IUL for the last twenty years received an average return of around 8% year over year. If you take an IUL and run it over a 20 to 30 year period anytime in the history of the market you will have a return of around 7%.

So how fast does your money double? The rule of 72. If we take 72 and divide by the interest rate we know how often your money doubles. So, for this illustration the Department of Insurance requires I use 5.5% (please check current regulation). 72 / 5.5 = 13 years. With your savings account at 1% interest it takes 72 years to double.

For those people who had an IUL in any of those hypothetical 20 to 30 year periods they doubled their money around every ten years. Now again I can't guarantee your money will double at this rate or the stock market will continue to grow at the same pace.

DJIA - Historical 1925 - 2016

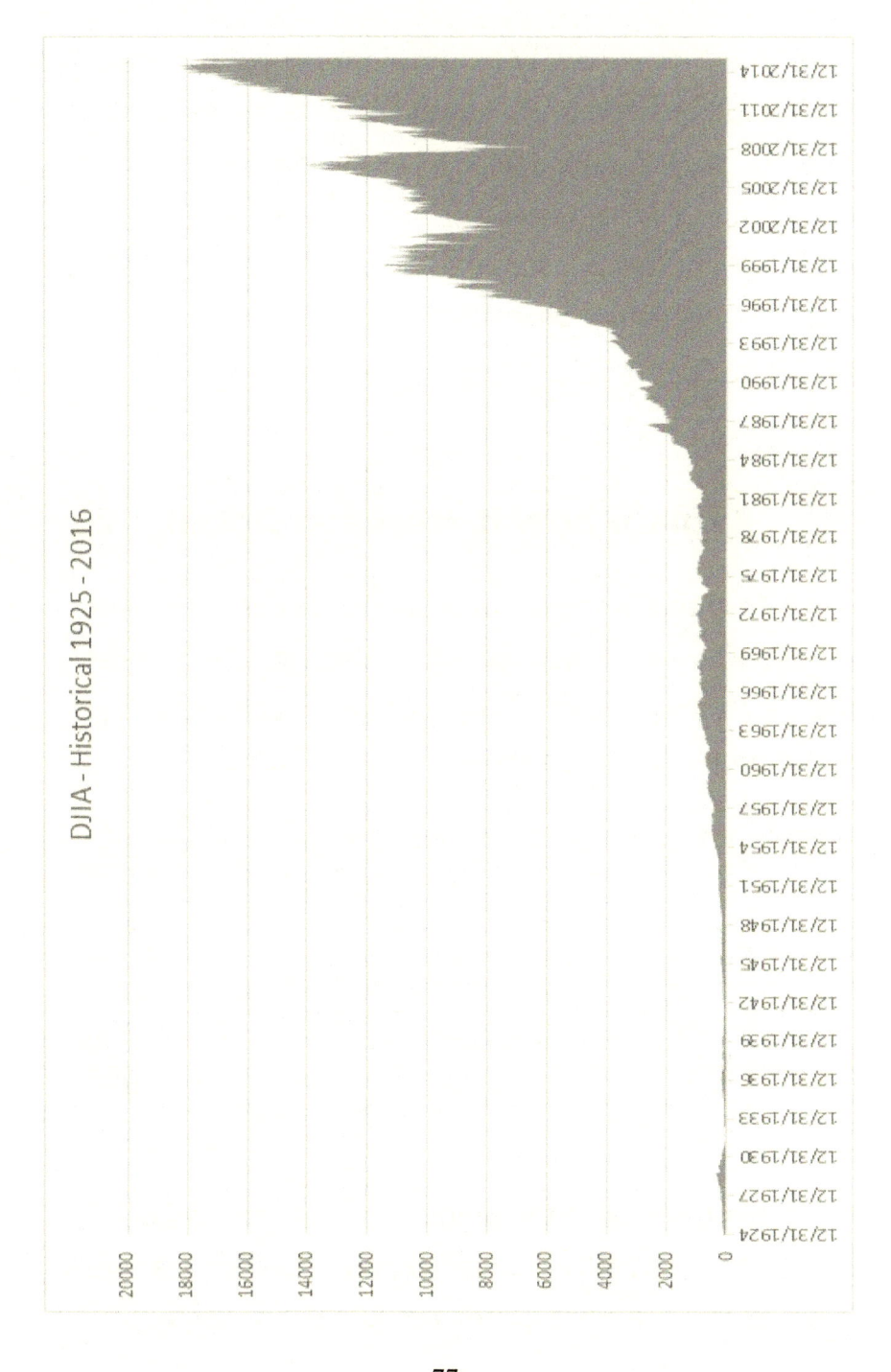

Note. The Department of Insurance set specific guidelines for illustrations and those guidelines were set for good reasons. So, it's always good to follow the guidelines set forth and learn the guidelines. Always check with your management team, insurance company compliance officer and attorney before presenting a SLIRP.

## Explain how it works in Detail.

Now that we know what an IUL/SLIRP does. Now we know how it hedges against tax uncertainty, against the uncertainty about social security and against those 4 major problems... Let's show you how it works.

| Year | Age | Premium | Withdrawal | Loan | Net Accumulated | Net Surrender | Death Benefit |
|---|---|---|---|---|---|---|---|
| 1 | 25 | $5,000 | 0 | 0 | 4000 | 500 | 1,000,000 |
| 2 | 26 | $5,000 | 0 | 0 | 10000 | 1200 | 1,000,000 |
| 3 | 27 | $5,000 | 0 | 0 | 12000 | 3500 | 1,000,000 |
| 4 | 28 | $5,000 | 0 | 0 | 20000 | 7655 | 1,000,000 |
| 5 | 29 | $5,000 | 0 | 0 | 25000 | 12000 | 1,000,000 |
| 6 | 30 | $5,000 | 0 | 0 | 30000 | 20000 | 1,000,000 |
| 7 | 31 | $5,000 | 0 | 0 | 35000 | 25000 | 1,000,000 |
| 8 | 32 | $5,000 | 0 | 0 | 40000 | 35000 | 1,000,000 |
| 9 | 33 | $5,000 | 0 | 0 | 47000 | 45777 | 1,000,000 |
| 10 | 34 | $5,000 | 0 | 0 | $50,000 | $50,000 | |
| Total | | $50,000 | | | | | |

Simply explain the premium to fund the policy. Explain the surrender charges in detail. Explain the break-even point. On a front loaded product the breakeven point is around 7 to 10 years.

| Year | Age | Premium Outlay | Withdrawal | Loan |
|---|---|---|---|---|
| 20 | 35 | $5,000 | 0 | 0 |
| 21 | 36 | $5,000 | 0 | 0 |
| 22 | 37 | $5,000 | 0 | 0 |
| 23 | 38 | $5,000 | 0 | 0 |
| 24 | 39 | $5,000 | 0 | 0 |
| 25 | 40 | | 25,000 | 0 |
| 26 | 41 | | 25,000 | 0 |
| 27 | 42 | | | 25,000 |

Explain how the distributions work and how the loan works. Explain how the premium outlays change and then how the death benefit changes as well. Make sure to talk about how the loan works and what the interest rate will be when taking out the loan. Explain how a wash loan works. Explain how the policy works in understandable simple terms. Explain how long we can estimate they take money out of the policy for and how the death benefit changes over time. If we design it correctly it fulfills the gap in the income goal we addressed earlier. Make sure not to gloss over the details.

Review the four major questions/problems for the second time. If everything was designed correctly as a supplement the IUL should help your client meet their age/income goals and meet the four concerns. From here you need to close the application.

## Closing the Sale

I've always found that the simple conversations seem to be the most effective as you don't dilute the close. Once you've explained how it works. Explain the application process and then just sell the application process. Stick to a simple analogy for how life insurance functions and how we need to apply for it.

Bob, a SLIRP is not like buying a bar of soap at a

grocery store. It's a process where we submit an application on your behalf and after some brief medical underwriting the life insurance company will make one of two choices based on your application, either the life company will make an offer or not make an offer.

It's kind of like applying for a job. Do you always get every job you apply for? Of course not. (Sell the application because until underwriting comes back with an offer it's all theoretical)

## Should we use an Increasing or level death benefit?

There are generally two types of Death Benefit Options that we can choose from for a permanent life insurance policy.

- Type A Level
- Type B Increasing

The first is commonly known as an A or level death benefit and the second is a B or increasing death benefit. The A option is purely the face amount on the policy and the B option is simply the death benefit plus the accumulated cash value of the policy. Generally speaking, this is one of those situations that will vary for each client and if you want to maximize potential gains then increasing is generally the best option as the upfront cost of insurance is less and allows for faster accumulation.

## Should we Overfund the policy?

It depends on the budget and the policy you end up going with. Generally, a target premium is an estimate because of cost of insurance increases and the fact we don't have a crystal ball to predict investment outcomes. So in general overfunding if allowable by the client is a good idea. To borrow a phrase from one of my early mentors, "To overfund is to properly fund an IUL." Again, this is one of those questions that doesn't have a binary cookie-cutter answer.

## When does a policy MEC? Modified Endowment Contracts

The simplest way to think about a MEC is that it will depend on the cash value in the policy. To determine when a policy will 'MEC' we use what is called the 7 Pay

Test. Basically, the cash surrender value cannot exceed a single premium or the death benefit has to be a certain percentage of premium within the policy. Your life insurance company will let you know the parameters when taking out the loan. Make sure to figure this out before helping a client take out the policy loan as it could mean huge tax consequences.

## What about Premium Financing?

A popular strategy for high net worth clients is utilizing premium financing to fund an IUL or VUL. The idea is rather simple, a loan is taken out to frontload the life insurance and the resulting high gains outweigh the interest rate on the loan. This methodology albeit sounding simple, in practice is extremely risky and complicated. **Consult an Attorney.**

## Do I need a life insurance trust LIT/ILIT?

The answer is that I don't know. The answer could be yes, no and or maybe. What I suggest is that you consult an attorney who specializes in estate planning or better yet team up with one. **Consult an Attorney.**

## Don't be 'that' guy.

Three years ago I was training a life insurance broker who was working on a case for a prospect. The prospect had an existing (IUL) life insurance contract with a large insurance company. The broker was working up numbers for the client as the client requested to shop. When I asked the broker why the broker simply replied, "Well, the client is paying too much for their IUL." To which I replied, "If that is the story you're getting, then how well do you think the client understands how an IUL is supposed to work?" If you keep switching contracts then all of your existing contract value will get depleted thru early withdrawals and penalties. An IUL only works if you understand compounding interest and the cost basis over the first 10 years. It's a front loaded product. As an insurance agent we have duties to advise in the best interest of the client, not our pocket books. Don't go around selling replacement contracts just to make a few bucks.

# Dealing with Stakeholders: Advisors, Accountants and Attorneys

Every time I watch my favorite financial advisor interview a life agent and debate term vs perm, it doesn't end well for the life agent. Why? Because, selling isn't telling, it's about asking questions. A considerable amount of my time as a life insurance agent was dealt handling objections from key stakeholders or people who tended to have the ear of my insured. Does this sound familiar? "Well Mike, this all sounds great but I really should run it by my Tax guy..." Or, "Well Mike, my CPA, my financial advisor told me I should always buy term and invest the rest." So, what do you do?

- When will my client die?
- Will my client have less debt, more debt, or the same proportion of debt over the next 30 to 40 years?
- How will my client avoid nursing care?
- How will our client avoid illnesses?

By recommending term insurance over a life time what are the financial consequences? Firstly, if you go with the term option what is your biggest risk? Well, you are forcing the client to at a minimum show insurability 6 times instead of a single time with a permanent policy. With a permanent policy when properly designed it can be self-funding, so theoretically you stop paying premiums. The worst part with the term option is that generally you become uninsurable for coverage after age 80. While the permanent option provides lifetime coverage.

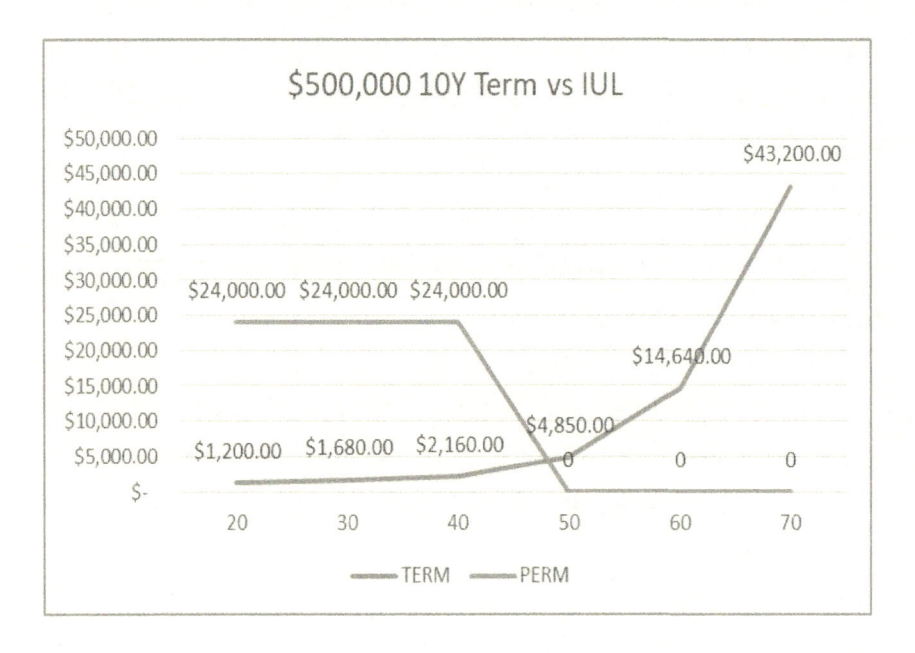

## $500,000 10Y Term vs IUL

| Age | TERM | PERM |
|-----|------|------|
| 20 | $1,200.00 | $24,000.00 |
| 30 | $1,680.00 | $24,000.00 |
| 40 | $2,160.00 | $24,000.00 |
| 50 | $4,850.00 | 0 |
| 60 | $14,640.00 | 0 |
| 70 | $43,200.00 | 0 |

What most advisors don't understand is that although term is much less expensive over a lifetime (in theory), you have to assume that the insured will not:

- Become Partially Disabled

- Become Permanently disabled
- Become critically ill
- Requite long term care
- Doesn't gain a significant amount of weight
- Has good blood pressure until age 70
- Has proper cholesterol until age 70
- Doesn't get any form of cancer
- Doesn't accumulate significant debt over time
- Doesn't accumulate significant assets over time
- Doesn't want to contribute to charity in large sums
- Enjoys paying high tax rates
- Doesn't lose eye sight
- Doesn't lose hearing
- Doesn't get into a life altering car accident
- Doesn't take medication until age 70
- Doesn't get surgery until age 70
- Doesn't smoke
- Doesn't vape
- Doesn't drink often
- Never has a felony
- Doesn't engage in dangerous sports activities

If you are reading this as a skeptical advisor, please tell me how many clients you've had who can meet that criteria. If you purchase a permanent product at an early age, the difference in lifetime premium is around $6000 to $10,000 over a LIFETIME! Assuming the policy is designed correctly and that the insured is young (Age 20) when the initial policy is purchased.

# Typical Newbie Mistakes

As a former newbie myself, I'd be lying if I told you I didn't make my share of mistakes. Know that most mistakes are correctable. Here are a few of the key mistakes that I notice life agents making on a regular basis:

- Presenting without Asking Questions
- Offering a recommendation too quickly
- Doesn't established self as an expert
- Neglects rapport building
- Not setting expectations for follow ups
- Not customizing the death benefit
- Switching out policies or swapping often aka replacement
- Re-routing funding from qualified plans to life insurance
- Not asking for permission to ask for the sale
- Not having a backup plan
- Not spending time to know the client

## Other Considerations

- An IUL/SLIRP is not a qualified plan. It's life insurance.
- Because the cost of insurance will most likely increase over time an IUL to be effective should be front loaded and over funded.
- Interest Rates on the loans are generally not guaranteed.
- Rate caps change and usually go down.
- An IUL is not a savings account.
- Surrender Charges in the first 10 years can be considerable.
- "Each policy will have a **"target premium"** payment. This **target** is the amount of **premium** that the insurance company believes to be adequate to fund the policy. It is generally a good idea to pay **premiums** at least equal to this **target premium.**" – **VCE**
- If you have securities licenses this presentation will have to be altered given what your insurance company compliance department

requires you not say and what you have to say a little differently. So check with your compliance officer before going this route. Even if you don't have securities license check with your compliance officer.
- Adapt this presentation and make it your own. Or pick something out of it that you find useful in it and use it.

# Other Sales Strategies

Life insurance sales strategies are not created equal. For as long as we have life agent we will have creative life sales strategies. In this part of the book we will cover some of those other strategies in very brief detail. Below are some of those strategies.

- LIRP – A Life Insurance Retirement Plan. Meant to be a larger scale version of a SLIRP used in accordance with a VUL or IUL.

- SLIRP

- Found Money – Providing other policies and or savings to divert into life insurance premiums.

- Premium Financing – Using a loan to fund a life insurance policy.

- Pension Maximization – Opting into single payee pension plan and using the differential between the second to die option to fund a life plan.

- Infinite Banking – Accumulating funds in an IUL to borrow against to pay your bills. This strategy is very interesting and I would recommend reading as much as possible about it.

- College Funding – Loan strategy to fund an IUL/VUL with the expectation of taking withdrawals around college time to pay for expenses.

- Mortgage Replacement – The idea behind this strategy is that the insured forgoes paying principal payments on a mortgage (interest rate of 5% or below) and uses that principal payment to invest in an IUL (up to 10% interest rate). With that IUL at the end of the mortgage theoretically the insured can pay for their mortgage and still have an outstanding balance of cash value in the insurance policy. The idea is that the interest rate of the life policy far outpaces the mortgage. This is probably the riskiest of all life strategies.

**\*Author Notation. These strategies are not my endorsement of the strategies just merely an educational explanation.**

# Index of Questions

- What will your tax rate be when you retire?
- Ideally, during the next twenty years until you retire, you want your money to do what?
- How would you like to pay?
- Have you considered paying in full if I could help you make more money?
- What do you do for a living?
- "Great! How'd you arrive at that amount of insurance?"
- Did you have an amount in mind or were you looking for some guidance?
- Would you prefer to leave your money to the government or leave it to your grandkids?
- What if you could your life insurance while you're alive?
- Where do you want to put your money?
- Do you want the government of your grandkids to get your money?
- With taxes at an all-time 100 year low and debt to GDP at an all-time 200 year high, where do you think taxes are going?

- Did you know that certain life insurance policies might put your children in a more favorable financial situation to obtain Federal Student Aid?
- What kind of investments do you have currently that are 100% market risk free?
- Do you have any investments that give you upside potential, eliminate downside market risk and provide you tax free distributions?
- Have you ever considered paying your insurance premium in full?
- John given your unique situation how often would you like to follow up and review your progress? Once a year? Twice a year?
- What do you have now that acts like life insurance?
- Do you have life insurance through your work? If so, how much?
- Who did you plan on having as the beneficiary of the policy?
- Have you recently applied for life insurance? If so, what was the outcome?

# Sales Rules

**Rule Number 1: Don't Complicate Something.**

Rule number one of selling insurance is to keep it simple. We are selling insurance not building a space ship. Explain the concepts in digestible terms that consumers can understand and stray away from using too much insurance jargon.

Once I sat thru a long sales consultation with a rep for a large life insurance company. The rep had a well thought out, but thoroughly confusing Indexed Presentation. After about 45 minutes of this rep carrying on I started wondering if she actually was going to talk about how the product actually worked or anything that might be relevant to product features

**Rule Number 2: Always be agreeable.**

Selling is as much an art as it is a science. There is no formula for agreeableness. Just know that the more confrontational the worse your odds are for closing. The customer is always right.

**Rule Number 3: Understand the Person.**

Don't make snap judgements about what someone can afford. Dig and discover what they can afford.

There are two types of people that sit in front of you. There are think type of people and feel type of people. What I mean is that people respond to questions in different ways. Some people say, "I think..." and some people say, "I feel..."

The reason why you need to grasp this concept, is the fact that during a sale we have these invisible boundaries. Emotional or feel people require stories and think people require figures and facts. Not everyone is the same. But, there is a limit for feel people and there is a limit for think people that we have to monitor in the sales process.

## Rule Number 4: The Person Needs to Understand you.

Ask yourself does the prospect have enough information to know, like and trust me? If not then you need to build that trust through conversation. Through asking questions.

## Rule Number 5: Reciprocity

If an insurance sale is a search for the truth we need to follow the rule of reciprocity. The rule of reciprocity makes the insurance buying process a collaborative effort not a confrontational one.

Remember you make no money until the person signs up with you, so you are educating them for free. This is the key to reciprocity. You ask questions to evoke emotions during the process and client has questions that you answer to provide certainty.

The reason why we focused so much on processes in this book is because each sale is more or less always going to be the same. It has an opening and a closing and in between you talk about stuff.

**Rule Number 6: Stick to a process.**

Every person is different, but every sale is exactly the same. In that, people give you the same responses, the same objections and will follow a path. When you start selling insurance it's important to remember that you have a start, you build rapport, you ask questions that are open ended, you find a problem if one exists, and you build a solution/close.

**Rule Number 7: Know When To Close and Know When to Fold.**

Some prospects believe it or not just enjoy talking

to sales people and have no intention of buying. Being a salesperson you must think that is somewhat crazy, I did. But, it's true.

During your presentation it's important to know when people are giving off buying signals and asking buying questions.

Think of a sale like a Turkey in the oven. First you have to marinate the turkey. Then you preheat the oven. After your prep work is complete and the oven is at the right temperature you put the Turkey in the oven.

Some turkeys require more prep work because some are FROZEN and some are fresh. You cook the turkey and check the temperature along the way. But, you have to keep marinating the turkey as it cooks. If the internal temperature is correct after X amount of hours you pull it out and it's moist. If you leave it in too long it dries out or maybe even burns or becomes ruined.

I'll make an effort to dispense with the food analogies for the rest of the book. Think of it this way.

Think of it like an index. The 'Closability' index. Some people are easier to close than others and some require a tremendous amount of effort. But, either way the prospect will ask buying questions.

Well, what's a buying question? For instance, "How much does this cost?" If you are not interested in a product you do not ask how much it will cost. Simple.

**Rule Number 8: Ask Open Ended Questions**

If you are new to sales or new to insurance. Your best friend is the ability to ask open ended questions and leading questions.

Would you mind if we talked about open ended questions? This is a directive question asking for permission to ask a question.

How do you feel about life sales? What do you think about life sales? Whatever the answer always remember to ask follow up questions. You have two ears and one mouth so as a ratio ask too questions before you start to babble on about insurance.

### Rule number 9: Set Expectations

You need to set boundaries. What should a client come to expect of you? What do you expect of a client? A lot of Agents (including myself) tell each client something to the extent of, "We meet with each client once per year to make sure the insurance is current or on target." There is nothing customized about that statement. Instead why not just ask. How often would you like to meet each year to discuss your insurance? Most of my clients find once a year to meet their needs but some prefer a call once a quarter to check in.

### Rule Number 10: Don't lose control of the conversation.

Probably the most common challenge for newer agents is not maintaining focus. A prospect is going to focus on price if you let them and it can derail the conversation.

Price is merely the cost of value. It's your job to educate and present the value. Remember you are the expert and what you focus on will direct the conversation. Don't avoid talking about price, but at the same time don't rush or lead with price. See Diagram Below.

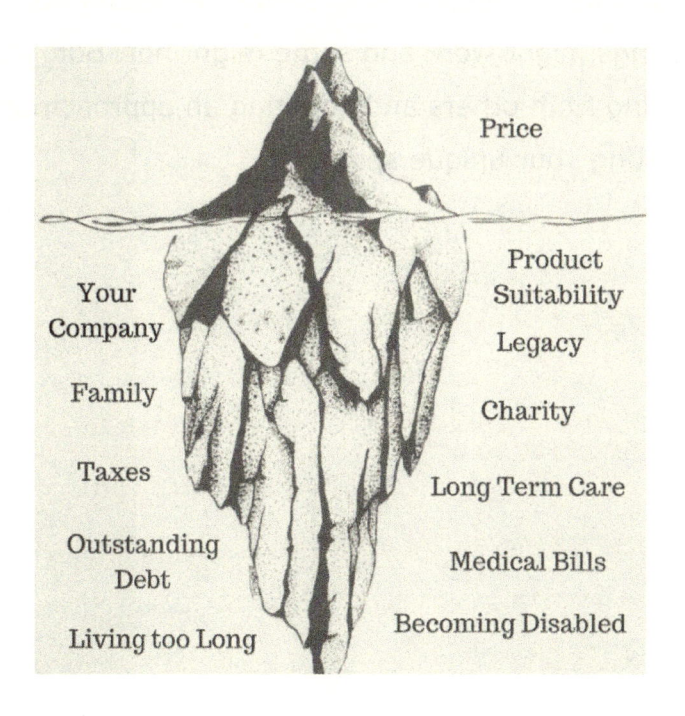

[Iceberg diagram: Above water - Price. Below water - Your Company, Family, Taxes, Outstanding Debt, Living too Long, Product Suitability, Legacy, Charity, Long Term Care, Medical Bills, Becoming Disabled]

**Rule Number 11: Don't always try to reinvent the**

**wheel.**

My father was a carpenter and used to say the nail that sticks out tends to get hammered. Craft your approach as you learn your trade. If your trade is selling insurance, then read, apply and learn. It's important as you craft your style/approach to make adjustments. Somethings might work and some might not. But, start by learning from others and adopting an approach and then putting your unique spin on it.

# Summation

Please share this book with a friend. If you have 30 seconds and you enjoyed this content please leave me a review so I can help spread more content to help Agents. Being an insurance agent is not an easy job. Whether you are a life insurance agent, multi-line agent, captive agency owner and or producer, this industry is changing and becoming hyper competitive. Distribution models are evolving and disrupting the insurance marketplace. Given the fact you've taken the time to read this book, I can confidently say that you are probably trying to make a real difference. Education is the one thing that once earned, no one can ever take away from you. Hopefully, you've learned, adopted, borrowed and or adapted your process after reading this.

Made in the USA
Coppell, TX
28 May 2022

78228768R00062